12

DIVINE COMEDY

GLEN SCRIVENER

10 Publishing
a division of 10 of those.com

DIVINE COMEDY

WHAT IS LIFE?

HUMAN TRAGEDY

OTHER BOOKS BY GLEN SCRIVENER:

321: The Story of God, the World and You

Four Kinds of Christmas

Love Story

Copyright © 2018 by Glen Scrivener

First published in Great Britain in 2018

British Library Cataloguing in Publication Data

A record for this book is available from the British Library

ISBN: 978-1-912373-18-5
Designed by Diane Warnes
Printed in Denmark by Nørhaven

10Publishing, a division of 10ofthose.com
Unit C, Tomlinson Road, Leyland, PR25 2DY, England
Email: info@10ofthose.com
Website: www.10ofthose.com

CONTENTS

TRAGEDY OR COMEDY?

You know how they categorize Shakespeare's
plays, right? If it ends with a wedding,
it's a comedy. And if it ends with a funeral,
it's a tragedy. So we're all living tragedies,
because we all end the same way,
and it isn't with a ... wedding.

ROBYN SCHNEIDER, *The Beginning of Everything*[1]

What is life: a tragedy or a comedy?

A lot depends on your definition. Mel Brooks
once said, 'Tragedy is when I cut my finger.
Comedy is when you fall into an open sewer and
die.' That's one perspective – not one I'll use in
this book though. I'm thinking of 'comedy' and
'tragedy' in a more technical sense.

I'm not asking whether life is a barrel of laughs.
We all know it's not. 'Comedy' and 'tragedy'
have particular meanings. In literature 'comedy'
and 'tragedy' refer to the shape of a story, not so
much its content, or even its tone.

Shakespeare's tragedies, for instance, were
full of jokes. Or at least that's what our English

teachers told us at school. If we're honest, we probably hadn't noticed the gags – I hadn't anyway. When the alleged 'humour' was pointed out, I dutifully said, 'Oh,' and wrote in my exercise book: 'Hamlet is making a joke, apparently.'

Tragedies can have jokes, and comedies can have heartache. In fact much of comedy depends upon the banana-peel moment, the pompous being brought down a peg or two, or the grand farce where everything falls apart.

Tragedies contain joy, comedies contain pain, but the distinguishing mark of both is the ending. At the end of a Shakespearean tragedy the bodies are piled up on the stage. At the end of a Shakespearean comedy – in fact in all 14 of them – there is a wedding. Or four.

To help you fix it in your mind, think of it this way: a comedy is shaped like a smile. You go down then up – descending into darkness before rising up to joy. A tragedy, on the other hand, is shaped like a frown – up then down. You climb to prosperity then tumble into the pit.

So now that we've clarified the question, let me ask it again. What is life: a tragedy or a comedy?

Tragedy, surely! That's what Professor Lawrence Krauss would tell us: 'The picture that science presents to us is … uncomfortable. Because what we have learned is that we are more insignificant than we ever could have imagined … And in addition it turns out that the future is miserable.'[2] We are the flotsam of a cosmic explosion and biological survival machines – wet robots – clinging to an insignificant rock, hurtling through a meaningless universe towards eternal extinction. Still, all that being said, the new flavoured latte from Starbucks is *incredible*. And have you tried hot yoga? We're renovating the kitchen too. So, you know, that's nice … As the annihilating tsunami of time bears down on us, we obsess over our sandcastles – the promotion, the holiday, the new gadget – and we dare not look up.

Life is a tragedy and this dismal tale is sold to us in every magazine and paperback: 'The thousand books you must read before you die'; 'The ten must-see destinations for your bucket list'. The shape of the story is *up* then *down* and the advertisers are primed to sell you the *uppiest up* that money can buy because the *down* really is a downer. The photographs are glossy, but they mask an unutterable tragedy. Life, according to the wisdom of the age, is about enjoying our brief 'moment in the sun'. We clamber upwards, grab for ourselves all the achievements, experiences and pleasures that we can and then, so soon, we are 'over the hill' and the grave awaits. It's up then down. The frowny face. The tragedy.

If you want proof that our culture tells a tragic tale about life, witness its obsession with youth. Since our story's ending is so bleak we focus on the beginning. On billboards we emblazon images of 17-year-old models who look like 12-year-old girls and who tell us how to fight the seven signs of ageing. Undeniably we have a cult of youth while at the same time we keep the elderly and the dying out of sight, out of mind. On my social media feeds the only time I hear of the elderly is when they act like young people. So, occasionally, there's the story of the 70-year-old marathon runner, or the 80-year-old break dancer or the 90-year-olds into speed dating. And we say, 'Aren't these old people inspiring …?' What we fail to add (but what we undeniably mean) is '… *when they act like 20-year-olds.*' We don't prize the elderly for the qualities traditionally associated with them: wisdom and experience. No. But when they muster up the vigour to ape our youthful trends, then we'll pay attention. Briefly.

We are constantly being distracted – and constantly distracting ourselves – from the end of our life's story. We are certain that life is a tragedy and so we focus on the beginning as much as possible. All the while though we are marching, inevitably, towards a 'miserable ever after'.

Then – against all the odds and in distinction to all its competitors – the Bible comes along and dares to tell a different story.

A UNIQUE STORY

There is no tale ever told that men would rather find was true, and none which so many sceptical men have accepted as true on its own merits.

J.R.R. TOLKIEN

The Bible is unique. It stands alone in the midst of the world's great religions and worldviews. It actually has the audacity to be a comedy. The story it tells holds out dazzling and eternal hope for us. While the religions of the East speak of dissolving into the ocean of being and while Islam and the Christian cults portray an otherworldly future, the Bible promises resurrection. This is different. It's about our bodies and our world being raised up. It's a tale of *this* life being laid hold of and turned around, like the plot twist in a classic comedy. Resurrection is about the author doing something joyous with our story – this one, the one we're in – taking us through the valley of the shadow and out into an improbable but thrilling finale. The Bible is a comedy and it all centres on Easter.

On the cross God's Son went down into the depths, entering a hell of a tragedy. But then, on Easter Sunday, the very one who went down into the grave came back up again. The one who died did not rot. Neither was he replaced. He was raised. And the Bible tells us that he is the pattern for what God will do with the whole world. God's *people* and God's *world* will be raised up. Not replaced, but renewed. Not consigned to the trash heap so God can start over elsewhere. No, resurrection is a happy ending, even for this careworn world, even for this tragic old life. The author of the story has stepped in to turn things around, to make our tragedy into his comedy.

This really is our one shot at the comedy. Lawrence Krauss has told us the secular story of a miserable ever after. The religions of the world offer, at best, a disembodied and unearthly paradise. There's only one story that turns out well for physical life on planet earth. This ought to be an incentive for us to investigate its truth.

But as we turn to the Christian story, we need to clear up an objection. You might be wondering whether Christians, with their 'happily ever after', are guilty of wish fulfilment? Are we clinging on to this story because we refuse to face facts? Is this just a comforting fantasy or is there something substantial in the Christian story – something solid to base our hopes on?

At the beginning of this chapter we have quoted J.R.R. Tolkien, author of *The Lord of the Rings*. He said, 'There is no tale ever told that men would rather find was true ...' Tolkien tells us that the Easter story is uniquely hopeful. But that's not all. It's also, he says, uniquely credible. He goes on, '... and none which so many sceptical men have accepted as true on its own merits.' This is not just wish-fulfilment. There is something about Christianity that is open to investigation. Sceptical men and women can explore its claims and affirm its truthfulness. How might that happen?

INVESTIGATING THE STORY

In this book we'll be exploring a short paragraph from the Bible. It's from a letter that the Apostle Paul wrote to a church in Philippi in about AD 62. Today we'd call that part of the world northern Greece. In it, as we shall see, Paul was probably quoting a song that the early Christians were singing. If it wasn't a song already, once Paul penned it, it would become a classic – the inspiration for hundreds more songs on the same theme. It's a true comedy, all about God's Son descending to the depths then rising to the heights. As we encounter its words, we have the opportunity to do some investigation.

The song, which was circulating very soon after the first Easter, makes a bold claim – one we can probe. It says that God has entered our world, endured our tragedy and risen again to bring us a glorious hope. If we doubt the people who swore by it, we can act like good detectives. If we think the originators of the story were lying, we can ask ourselves what was their *motive*, their *means* and their *opportunity* to commit the crime?

Perhaps you're familiar with motive, means and opportunity? I haven't studied law; I've just watched enough crime dramas to have picked up the concept. Look it up yourself! If a court is going to find you guilty of a crime, they need to establish your 'motive' (your reason for doing it), your 'means' (your resources that would enable you to commit the crime) and your 'opportunity' (could you have been there at the right time, in the right place?). If we think that Christians just invented the story of Jesus being God, dying and then rising again, we can ask:

WHAT WAS THEIR MOTIVE?

Christians were persecuted intensely for clinging to this story. The Jews couldn't stand their claim that Jesus was the long-promised Saviour, the Messiah. The Romans couldn't stand their insistence that Jesus, not Caesar, was Lord. This story did not win them any friends. Many Christians paid for their adherence to Jesus with their lives. The only reason they clung to this story is because they thought it was inescapably true.

WHAT WERE THEIR MEANS?

The early Christians were the scum of the earth, the dregs of society. They had no worldly power. They were not 'the winners' who could rewrite the history books, nor could they 'control the narrative' in the broader culture. They were losers. Yet their story, just on its own terms, turned the world upside down.

WHAT WAS THEIR OPPORTUNITY?

Some suggest that the story of Jesus became embellished over the years. Perhaps, in due course, people began to think of their great leader as a God. Maybe, generations later, his followers started telling tales of how the grave could not hold him, and so on. Yet there was no time for such legends to develop. This bold teaching from the early Christians, like in the song that we're studying, came much too early to make the 'embellishment' theory work. You need to wait till the eye-witnesses are long dead before you start monkeying with the story. The first Christians had no such opportunity to embroider the facts.

So the Easter story spread quickly, it comes from the powerless and it comes from a people who gain nothing materially from its telling. This story goes onto grip the world and it births history's greatest sociological phenomenon – the church. It builds civilisations and founds our greatest institutions, our schools and universities, our hospitals, modern science, economics – the list goes on. There is something out of this world about this story and yet it's a story that has *built* our world.

None of these factors prove that the words we're about to study are from God – God will have to assure you of that as you read! – but you should at least take these words with the utmost seriousness. Here is a story that bears all the hallmarks of truth.

You have every reason to *want* this to be true and you have every reason to *find* this to be true. My prayer is that you would join Tolkien, myself and billions of others in celebrating the beauty *and* the truthfulness of this unique comedy.

ENTERING THE TRAGEDY

The happy ending is justly scorned as a misrepresentation; for the world, as we know it ... yields but one ending: death.

JOSEPH CAMPBELL, *The Hero with a Thousand Faces*[3]

The biggest problem in trying to convince you that life is a comedy is that you live on planet earth. Maybe if you'd grown up on some other planet, you could swallow the whole 'happily ever after' caper. Unfortunately we live among death, disease and disasters and, naturally enough, we find it hard to believe in happy endings. The ancient Greeks thought of tragedies as 'high art' and comedies as 'low art'. They reckoned that tragedies were truthful engagements with the world as it is. Comedies, on the other hand, were considered to be frivolous escapes from life's harsh realities. Even today Oscars for Best Picture are much more likely to be awarded to dramas than comedies. We struggle to believe that there's much depth or reality to comedies.

If I'm going to persuade you to believe in the divine comedy, I'll have to show you that it's a *realistic* comedy. I need to demonstrate that it takes in the pain and the darkness of this world. You will have to know that this is not escapism, but rather a true engagement with life in the trenches. Thankfully that's exactly the kind of comedy that Easter proclaims. Here is the first half of our song from the Apostle Paul:

In your relationships with one another, have the same mindset as Christ Jesus:

who, being in very nature God,

did not consider equality with God something to be used to his own advantage;

rather, he made himself nothing

by taking the very nature of a servant,

being made in human likeness.

And being found in appearance as a man,

he humbled himself

by becoming obedient to death –

even death on a cross!

PHILIPPIANS 2:5–8

Our story begins on high. Comedies typically do – remember the 'smile' shape. We start the song by considering our ancient origins. Wind back the clock before the world began and what do you find? Christ Jesus! Perhaps that's a shock. People tend to think of Jesus as inventing a religion. The Bible insists that he first invented the universe. According to the Bible, Jesus is the eternal Son of God, filled by the life-giving Spirit – and he always has been. Long before he joined the human race, he was 'in very nature God'. If you picture God's life like a fountain, the Father has forever been pouring out his Spirit on to and in to Jesus, his Son. Jesus has always been in on this eternal fountain of life, light and love.

If you've heard the word 'Trinity', that's what's in view here. God is a tri-unity, a unity of three: the Father, the Son and the Holy Spirit. Jesus is the Son and therefore 'in very nature God'.

But what does he do with all that 'God-ness'? Answer: he plunges to the depths! The one who is 'in very nature God' takes the 'very nature of a servant'. And that's just the beginning. The Son who became a servant kept on stooping all the way to sacrifice – all the way to a shameful, godforsaken crucifixion. This might be a comedy, but it's the most blood-soaked comedy imaginable. From heavenly heights God's Son has descended to the depths. He didn't just meet us in our pit; he threw himself under our feet. He didn't merely stoop to our station; he plunged far beneath it, to a hell of a life and a hell of a death. No-one volunteers for crucifixion. No-one except Jesus. The one who was 'in very nature God' chooses to become the one with his arms nailed open, bleeding for the world. As the song says, this was his 'mindset' from the beginning. The cross is what expresses his divine nature.

Here is perhaps the deepest truth I know – I wonder whether it's the deepest truth there is: when Jesus died on the cross, he was not taking a holiday from being God. He didn't leave all that 'God stuff' in heaven while he did the 'cross stuff' on earth. The 'cross stuff' was the purest expression of the 'God stuff'. The cross is what it looks like when God shows up.

WHAT DOES IT LOOK LIKE WHEN GOD SHOWS UP?

I once preached a sermon with that title. I was a visiting speaker at a new church and they decided to do some publicity – flyers and a poster. During the week people asked me, 'Have you seen the publicity for Sunday?' I hadn't. But I didn't think anything more of it until I showed up on the morning of the service. Outside the church stood a giant billboard with the title: 'What does it look like when God shows up?' The trouble was that next to the question was a massive picture of *me*. At best the passers-by would have read the poster and been hugely disappointed. At worst they would have been outraged at the blasphemy. God does not look like *me*! Yet the truth of the cross is even more scandalous than that poster. The truth is that God looks like Jesus dying on the cross. In fact there's never been a better angle on God than the view of the Good Friday crowd. They thought they were witnessing a public execution; actually they were encountering divine revelation. The cross was God's grand unveiling.

So what does it look like when God shows up? Apparently it looks like the cross! The Bible passage from which I was preaching that morning came from Paul's letter to a church in Corinth. It begins with the teaching that God's power and wisdom are shining at full strength when we see Jesus dying in agony (see 1 Corinthians 1:17–25).

How can that be? It sounds crazy, but actually it makes sense. If, as we've said, God is like a fountain of life, then where do we see a fountain most clearly? We see it when it is poured out. So when do we see the very 'God-ness' of God?

Answer: when he is poured out in death. With every drop of his lifeblood Jesus gives of himself, even to death, 'even death on a cross'. It sounds contradictory, but actually it's not. The Fountain is revealed in the outpouring. When we see *his death*, really we are seeing *God's life*. Picture the cross. No-one has ever witnessed divine glory like the glory of that sacrifice.

In fact when you truly grasp Jesus' death, you start to doubt anyone else's claims to deity. Jesus is the God who has stooped to save. Why hasn't anyone else shown up in our pit? In some religions the gods do occasionally come down to earth. (Unlike Jesus they never enter into our history, our time and space; it's always in a mythological dream time). Yet such gods are, typically, not loving or noble enough to die for their people. Most often they are characters beset with the same selfishness as us. In other religions the gods are far off and distant. They would never stoop to heaven, let alone earth, let alone the cross. But on the cross we see the true God – the Fountain who would pour himself out for his people. The cross, far from casting doubt on Jesus' 'God-hood', is the highest proof of his deity.

The true God is the God of the cross – the one showing up in our tragedy.

THE VIEW FROM BELOW

Man is his own worst enemy.

MARCUS TULLIUS CICERO

On 22 September 2017 Clayton and Brittany Cook were tying the knot in Kitchener, Ontario. You may have heard of them. Their post-wedding photograph has now gone viral, but not because they looked picture perfect. Clayton actually looks like a drowned rat – a very well-dressed drowned rat, admittedly. If you search for the pic, you will see his white rose still in its place, buttoned to his royal-blue jacket. But he looks like he's just taken a dip in a muddy river. That's because he has. Not very befitting a bridegroom, you might think. This is exactly what his new bride thought: 'I looked over at the river and it looked like he was in the water taking a swim and I was like oh my gosh, what are you doing?' Actually he was saving a life.

Some kids had been playing near the river while the photographer was taking solo shots of Brittany. One of them fell in. No-one saw except Clayton. So he dived in. He saved the kid and emerged again, the photographer turning just in time to take the viral image. Without the context you might think, 'Not a great look for a bridegroom.' With the context you shout, 'Hero!'

It's the same with Jesus' crucifixion. You might look at the cross and think, 'Not a great look for a God!' But when you understand the context, everything changes. When you see that Jesus' clothes were not just sullied, they were stripped; he didn't just get muddy, he got bloody; he didn't just risk his life, he gave it …; when you realise there were no photographers to capture the bravery, no wider audience applauding the act, just a solitary man giving everything to save the unworthy, you cry out, 'What a Hero! What a Saviour! What a God!'

SEEING JESUS – SEEING OURSELVES

When you see the cross in its true context, you start to view things differently. You see Jesus differently, but you also see yourself in a new light. You begin to realise that you are someone in need of rescue.

I remember walking through Kaduna in northern Nigeria on a baking hot afternoon. I'd been to the market and was making my way back to the school where I was doing some teaching. Suddenly I felt a hand grab me tightly around my wrist. 'Not that way, sir!' I turned to see one of my students. His eyes were wide. 'That's not safe for you,' he said, and I believed him. I hadn't heard of Boko Haram at the time, but soon I would read of horrifying atrocities committed by people from that very neighbourhood.

Before my student stopped me, I was happily sauntering in the African heat. Now, from the look he was giving me, I felt as though I'd been saved from danger. I really had been.

It can be like that when we view the cross. We can be happily sauntering through life, unaware of the dangers, but all of a sudden we see a Saviour with blood-earnest urgency. It's the ultimate 'Not that way!' At the cross we see a rescuer who takes our plight with a seriousness we'd never considered. As he stretches out his arms to save us, we need to reconsider our situation. Apparently we're in trouble. Real trouble. Jesus has dived in to rescue us. As we see what he endured – godforsaken death – we need to understand that this must be the plight that we should expect. The hell he takes on the cross is the hell that we would otherwise face.

How can this be? Well we have to do business with the difference between ourselves and God. We live in God's world, but we ourselves are incredibly 'ungodly'. He is a Fountain of light, life and love but we, on the other hand, have rejected the light and so have entered darkness; we have turned from life, and so have entered death; we have turned from love, and so have entered disconnection. Every boast we make, every lie we tell, every lust we indulge, every slander we unleash, every grudge we bear testifies to a life lived in estrangement from God. This darkness – the Bible calls it sin – is proof that we're alienated from God. And if we're alienated from God, the life-source, what else can we expect but godforsaken death? This is the problem Jesus comes to solve: the problem of our sin.

Those boasts, lies, lusts, slanders and grudges are a kind of hell in miniature that bursts out of us. When we commit these sins, we'll often say, 'I don't know what came over me.' Of course nothing came over us. It all came out of us – out of a place that is deep, dark and diseased. If this spiritual sickness is not healed, it will degenerate continually. That's hell in its fullness.

You might baulk at such an idea. In many ways I'd be surprised if you didn't – no-one likes to be told bad news. But if you doubt the seriousness of our plight, I'd simply ask you to look again at the cross. Ask yourself, 'Why is Jesus there?' Clearly he thinks we're in trouble or he wouldn't go to such lengths. Will you allow the Rescuer to inform you of your plight? And then will you allow the Rescuer to do his rescuing? It's why he came.

The God of light says, 'I will take your darkness on myself'; the God of life says, 'I will take your death on myself'; the God of love says, 'I will take your disconnection on myself.' That's what love does – love enters in to face the plight of the beloved. On the cross Jesus is loving us to hell and back. He's facing what we ought to face, in our name and on our behalf.

Like an almighty Clayton Cook, Jesus entered the pit that we have made for ourselves. He saved us by taking its consequences on himself. But Jesus does more than plunge down to our depths. He actually blasts a hole through that pit to bring us to something beyond it. Beyond the tragedy there is comedy.

THE TURNING POINT

If you're going through hell, keep going.

WINSTON CHURCHILL

In the 15th century the southern tip of Africa was called the 'Cape of Storms'. Throughout the 1400s dozens of attempts to round the cape had been dashed on those forbidding rocks. Thousands of lives had been lost, all of them trying to reach the 'promised land' of India by sea. With the spices of the Orient beckoning, many expeditions were launched, but all of them were swallowed by the storms. The cape seemed an impossible barrier which no-one could cross. That is until Vasco da Gama, the Portuguese explorer, made the attempt.

In July 1497 da Gama led a fleet of four ships from Lisbon, and by Christmas he had sailed through the storms and out the other side. He pioneered the trade route to India, and came back with spices to make himself and his whole kingdom rich. From Portugal to India and back again was a distance far further than a circumnavigation of the globe. It was, up until that time, the longest sea voyage ever attempted without sight of land. The journey was thought to be impossible. Yet as soon as it was accomplished, da Gama renamed the peninsula that had formerly thwarted all explorers. He called it the 'Cape of Good Hope'.

Easter is like a cosmic version of da Gama's exploits. It's about one man who endured the storms and opened up hope for us all. On the cross Jesus entered storms too strong for every other traveller along the route. Yet Jesus went through them and emerged into a 'promised land' – a resurrection life which he offers to all. Easter is what turns the deadly storms into good hope.

BREAK ON THROUGH TO THE OTHER SIDE

Therefore God exalted him to the highest place
   and gave him the name that is above every name.
PHILIPPIANS 2:9

When God's Son breathed his last on the cross, it was not the final gasp of a tragic hero. It was, rather, the trial that leads to triumph. When Jesus died, he was entering the storms of judgement and death as a pioneer – an almighty Vasco da Gama. Jesus was not a victim falling helplessly into the grave, nor was he a tourist 'dipping his toe' into death. Sometimes people speak disparagingly about Jesus' sacrifice, wondering how Jesus' death amounted to anything more than a 'lousy weekend' for the Son of God. But this is to misunderstand both death and Jesus.

Death is a realm. It's the pit we've been consigned to in our rebellion against God. As we saw in chapter three, we all turn our backs on the God of life, light and love. Therefore we are justly and understandably left with death, darkness and disconnection. This disconnection is what the Bible describes as hell – an outer darkness of estrangement from God and all his goodness. In a sense there is a hell – a disconnection – to be felt now, at least in part. But the real tragedy is that this disconnection, if left unhealed, will continue and deteriorate beyond our physical death. The true horror of death is not the ceasing of our heartbeats. Death is our 'Cape of Storms', a hell of a trap from which no-one should emerge.

But Jesus is a Saviour – a Pioneer to sail through the storms. He did not merely visit the realm of death. On the cross he entered death more fully than anyone ever has or could. Everyone else is like those shipwrecked sailors, swallowed by the storms. Those explorers had, in fact, never experienced the *fullness* of the storms. They had perished at the first onslaught of the elements. None of them knew the force of what da Gama and his fleet would endure. Only the pioneer could truly be said to know the fury of the 'Cape of Storms'. So it is with Jesus. Far from 'dipping his toe' into death, Jesus plunged into hell on Good Friday. He experienced the judgement of God more than anyone ever could. Not even Satan himself will know the depths of hell the way Jesus did on that cross.

Yet precisely because of Christ's work, as the Apostle Paul goes on to write in his letter to the church in Philippi, 'Therefore God exalted him to the highest place'. Through Good Friday we reach Easter Sunday. Out of the empty tomb came our Pioneer, proclaiming to the world, 'The storms are vanquished, the new world is opened, hope has arrived.'

J.R.R. Tolkien was so taken by this moment of victory he invented a word to describe it. He called Easter a 'eucatastrophe', that is a *good* catastrophe. He wrote,

The Resurrection was the greatest 'eucatastrophe' possible ... and produces that essential emotion:

Christian joy which produces tears because it is qualitatively so like sorrow, because it comes from those places where Joy and Sorrow are at one, reconciled, as selfishness and altruism are lost in Love.

Jesus' resurrection on Easter Sunday is a glorious interruption, upending all our expectations. It's an asteroid of pure joy landing in the midst of our sorrow. And precisely because it's an unexpected clash of comedy and tragedy, it provokes in us an awesome joy, a tear-filled wonder. It connects with the deepest reaches of the human soul.

The cross-scarred Victor returns from the fight and declares his love. He has, in fact, loved us to hell and back. Now, in the midst of our trials and pain, we are given a hope that we have not earned and a joy that we cannot repay. It's the stuff of fairy tales. Except that this fairy tale has come true.

In this context we read of God giving to Jesus 'the name that is above every name'. Essentially this is God saying to the world, 'Look at my Son! He is what it looks like to be God.' *Because* he endured hell, *therefore* he is the Prince of heaven. *Because* he poured himself out, *therefore* he reveals the Fountain. *Because* he endured the storms, *therefore* he is our hope.

HAPPILY EVER AFTER

A tragedy is a tragedy, and at the bottom, all tragedies are stupid ... Any fool with steady hands and a working set of lungs can build up a house of cards and then blow it down, but it takes a genius to make people laugh.

STEPHEN KING

In 2006 Monty Python's *Life of Brian* was voted the greatest comedy of all time by viewers of Channel 4. I can understand why. The writing and performances are exquisitely crafted. I've often used excerpts from the film in sermons because their skewering of the pomposity and absurdity of human religion harks back strongly to the biblical prophets. It harks back to Jesus himself. Jesus was constantly making fun of the 'religious'. (See Matthew 6 or Matthew 23 for some scorching takedowns of the first-century 'Bible-thumpers'.)

In its day though *Life of Brian* drew howls of outrage from many religious conservatives. Bishops appeared on television in their finery to denounce the film and its makers. But I think they may have objected to the wrong thing. Sharp humour is not a problem, or at least it shouldn't be for those who have read their Bibles. Sharp humour directed at religion is not a problem either. In fact religion is the chief target of satire in the Bible. Those aspects of *Life of Brian* should have been welcomed and celebrated.

Nevertheless there is still a problem with *Life of Brian*. The problem is not that the film is a comedy. The problem is that the film is *not* a comedy. It contains moments of pure hilarity, but it is unquestionably a tragedy. The hero, Brian, is constantly mistaken for Jesus, and he ends up, like the true Messiah, crucified. But for Brian there is no resurrection, no rescue, no happily ever after. Instead there is a chorus of the crucified singing, 'Always look on the bright side of death, just before you draw your terminal breath.' These are not the words of a comedy. In fact you could not find more quintessentially tragic lines than the ones that end the film: 'Life is quite absurd and death's the final word.'

I submit that *Life of Brian* should be voted one of the all-time great films. But it is not a great comedy. It is, instead, a great tragedy. And I mean that in every sense. If you follow its lead, you may laugh. You may laugh loud. But you won't laugh long.

By contrast our ancient song from the Bible gives a happy ending to take our collective breaths away:

... that at the name of Jesus every knee should bow,
    in heaven and on earth and under the earth,
and every tongue acknowledge that Jesus Christ is Lord,
    to the glory of God the Father.
PHILIPPIANS 2:10–11

The scene here is a grand finale that would tax Hollywood's greatest special effects departments. We are here taken beyond the victory of Easter to the very last day of history as we know it. All people from all times and places are gathered together as Jesus returns to bring in his resurrection future. As he is revealed, humanity's billions are flattened before his uncreated glory.

If you saw the scene on film, you could zoom in amidst the masses of prostrate worshippers and you would find yourself. Perhaps you're surprised to imagine yourself there – to imagine yourself bowing. You're not the bowing type, you think. But on this day you won't be able to stop yourself falling on your face in awe. Perhaps you've had an experience of meeting a hero of yours in real life.

Even small doses of human glory can turn us into a quivering wrecks. What about encountering God? What about meeting the Hero of Heroes?

When you see the Author of life stepping back on to centre stage, your knees will buckle, your limbs will hang loose, your jaw will drop, breath will be pressed from your lungs and the word 'Lord' will fly from your lips. You won't be able to do anything else, nor will the atheist next to you, nor the Buddhist next to her, nor the Muslim next to him. 'Every knee' will bow. 'Every tongue' will confess that Jesus Christ is Lord.

For those who gladly confess that Jesus is Lord, they will be raised up to feasting joy. For others, who still do not want this Light, they will cower away in the outer darkness. But it's Jesus that will be revealed as Lord. It's his kind of life that will be vindicated, his kind of future that will be *the* future. The plotline of history is a comedy. The only question is will we embrace reality the way that Jesus has defined it? He *is* Lord. His world *will* follow the divine comedy. There *will be* a happily ever after. But will we, personally, fall in line with ultimate reality? Or will we resist the comedy and persist in living the tragedy?

FROM TRAGEDY TO COMEDY

**The world is a comedy to those that think;
a tragedy to those that feel.**

HORATIO WALPOLE, 4th Earl of Orford

By nature we all live out the tragedy. Our day-to-day lives are about clambering up in the world, grasping at all the experiences and achievements we can. We do this driven by the drumbeat of fear – fear that soon we will lose it all when the grave claims us. This is the shape of our lives and it is the classic pattern of the tragedy: up and then down.

Yet when Jesus came, his very first words in Mark's gospel were these:

The time has come ... The kingdom of God has come near. Repent and believe the good news!
MARK 1:15

The word Jesus uses for 'repent' means, most literally, 'change your mind'. You *had* believed in bad news – you had believed that there was no Saviour, no way through the Cape of Storms – and you had lived accordingly. You had lived out the tragedy, believing that, when it comes to living the good life, it was down to you. With that mindset you thought of God as the problem and yourself as the solution.

But no, says Jesus, you should repent. You need a revolution of thinking that will revolutionise your life. God is not the problem and you are not the solution. You are the problem. God is the solution. Think again. Repent.

RENOUNCING THE TRAGEDY

Horace Walpole's words began this chapter: 'The world is a comedy to those that think; a tragedy to those that feel.' That is absolutely right. If we simply react emotionally to the sorrows of this world, we will instinctively call life a tragedy. But if we think again, we will see that even those sorrows bear the character of a comedy.

Everything that hurts so horrifically in this world hurts because it is not the way it's supposed to be. Every heartache is an instance of something that was originally good but later has been spoiled. It's health destroyed by disease, order wrecked by chaos, love ruined by hatred. All our pain is about something wonderful falling into catastrophe. Yet that *is* the shape of a comedy, at least the first half of it. Think! Even our sorrows testify to the comedy.

So Jesus tells us not simply to feel. We are to think again. Look at the world, look at him and then ask yourself, 'Might he be the answer to this fall? Might he be the One to turn it around?' If we start to think, 'Yes', then we are beginning to repent, beginning to renounce the tragedy.

And that leads us to the second part of Jesus' two-fold command: 'believe'. Actually you cannot do the first part – repenting – without, at the same time, doing the second part – believing. Repenting and believing are different angles on the same basic response. As you renounce the tragedy, you are also embracing the comedy.

EMBRACING THE COMEDY

All throughout the Old Testament, God had been preparing his people for the great comedy. The 'kingdom' was promised in which death would be defeated and self-giving love would reign supreme. When Jesus arrived on the scene, he said, 'The wait is over!' The kingdom has come because the King has arrived. Therefore, says Jesus, stop believing the tragedy and start believing in good news!

How should we do that? It happens by looking to Jesus. As you read the Bible, as you hear the good news proclaimed in church, as you wrestle through these issues with Christian friends and as you ask God in prayer, you are in the process of 'looking' to Jesus. All the while the question should be: 'Is he Lord?' In particular, look to the Easter events and ask yourself, 'Does his death seem like a tragedy or might it be the great turning point? Is he a tragic hero in a losing cause, or is he an unconquerable pioneer, blasting through death and out into cosmic hope?' If you start to see that it's the latter, then you are starting to embrace the comedy. You are repenting and believing the good news.

What will this mean? It will mean a number of joyful realisations that will work their way through the entirety of your life:

1. **Jesus is Lord.** He really is what God is like!
2. **The tragedy is a lie.** I don't need to live it a second longer!
3. **The comedy is true.** It really is going to be OK!

Of course that final truth needs putting in context. It's *going* to be OK ... *in the end*. In the short term the comedy will mean we actually descend into the valley. And perhaps we will descend far further than we had expected. As we follow Jesus as Lord, we follow the great Sufferer and Sacrificer, and he will call us to suffer and to sacrifice too, as we follow his way of self-giving love. Jesus is the one poured out, therefore embracing his kind of life will mean receiving from him and pouring ourselves out along the same path.

In Paul's letter to the Philippians that is exactly how he applies the truth of the song we've been looking at. As soon as he shares this song, he calls us to 'work out' our salvation which God has given us (verse 12), to 'shine' out our hope to a world darkened by bitterness (verse 15) and to 'hold' out words of life when tempted to keep silent (verse 16). Our lives, like Paul's, are to be 'poured out' in service to others (verse 17). This is the outgoing life of the comedy. *Because* we've embraced the comedy, therefore we serve, we sacrifice and we suffer. We used to climb up in the world, to grab at life selfishly. We've renounced that now. The path is down and then up. We give our lives away to others and find that we're enjoying *real* life – the life of the comedy.

None of this is the price of our salvation. Our salvation is absolutely free. Serving and sacrificing is not the price of salvation; it's the shape – the shape of the divine comedy. It's the way of true and lasting joy.

DO YOU GET IT?

So what do you think? You have heard something of the good news. Has anything fallen into place for you? Do you 'get it'?

Perhaps you have seen enough of Jesus to conclude that he is indeed Lord. And perhaps you are ready to renounce the selfish ways of the tragedy and to embrace Christ's way of the comedy.

Jesus said, 'The time has come ... The kingdom of God has come near. Repent and believe the good news!' Perhaps you'd like to do just that. Let me offer some words that you might want to pray in response to all this. You could say something like:

Dear God,

The world is full of tragedy, and at times it's too much. I admit though that I contribute to the tragedy with my own selfishness and sin. I'm sorry.

Thank you so much for Jesus. Thank you that he entered into our suffering and that he took my sin on the cross. Thank you that he rose again to give me hope.

I want the Lord Jesus in my life. Please fill me with his Spirit. And please may he lead me along his path of self-giving love and into your great happy ending.

In Jesus' name,

Amen.

If you want to learn more about following Jesus, please talk to the person who gave you this book or write to me: **glen@speaklife.org.uk**

You can also discover more about following Jesus at **www.three-two-one.org**

NOTES

[1] Robyn Schneider, *The Beginning of Everything* (Katherine Tegen Books, 2013).

[2] See the YouTube video 'Lawrence Krauss: Our Godless Universe is Precious' (https://www.youtube.com/watch?v=SB5cBl2np-I).

[3] Joseph Campbell, *The Hero with a Thousand Faces* (first published by Pantheon Books, 1949).

NOTES

10 Publishing
a division of 10 of those.com

10Publishing is the publishing house of **10ofThose**.
It is committed to producing quality Christian
resources that are biblical and accessible.

www.10ofthose.com is our online retail arm selling
thousands of quality books at discounted prices.

For information contact: **sales@10ofthose.com**
or check out our website: **www.10ofthose.com**